D1234475

DAVID MAMET

FAUSTUS

David Mamet was born in Chicago in 1947. He studied at Goddard College in Vermont and at the Neighborhood Playhouse School of Theater in New York. He has taught at Goddard College, the Yale School of Drama, and New York University, and lectures at the Atlantic Theater Company, of which he is a founding member. He is the author of the plays *The Cryptogram*, *Oleanna*, *Speed-the-Plow*, *Glengarry Glen Ross*, *American Buffalo*, and *Sexual Perversity in Chicago*. He has also written screenplays for such films as *House of Games* and the Oscar-nominated *The Verdict*, as well as *The Spanish Prisoner*, *The Winslow Boy*, *Spartan*, and *Wag the Dog*. His plays have won the Pulitzer Prize and the Obie Award.

ALSO BY DAVID MAMET

FAUSTUS

FAUSTUS

∎ ∎ ∎
∎ ∎ ∎

DAVID MAMET

VINTAGE BOOKS

A DIVISION OF RANDOM HOUSE, INC.

NEW YORK

A VINTAGE ORIGINAL, JULY 2004

Copyright © 2004 by David Mamet

Library of Congress Cataloging-in-Publication Data
Mamet, David.
Faustus : a play / David Mamet.
p.   cm.
"A Vintage original"—T.p. verso.
ISBN 1-4000-7648-X (trade pbk.)
1. Faust, d. ca. 1540—Drama.   I. Title: Faustus.
II. Title.
PS3563.A4345D7 2004
812'.54—dc22   2003064506

Book design by Robert Bull

www.vintagebooks.com

Printed in the United States of America
10 9 8 7 6 5 4 3 2 1

*This play is dedicated
to Colin Stinton*

FAUSTUS

PRODUCTION NOTES

Faustus received its world premiere on February 28, 2004, at The Magic Theatre, San Francisco. Chris Smith, Artistic Director; David Gluck, Managing Director.

Faustus	David Rasche
Magus	Dominic Hoffman
Wife	Sandra Lindquist
Friend	Colin Stinton
Boy	Benjaman Beecroft; Nathan Wexler

Director	David Mamet
Set Designer	Peter Larkin
Lighting Designer	Russell H. Champa
Costume Designer	Fumiko Bielefedt
Assistant Director	Emily Halpern
Magic Consultant	Deceptive Practices; Ricky Jay and Michael Weber

THE CHARACTERS

FAUSTUS

HIS WIFE

HIS FRIEND

A MAGUS

FAUSTUS'S SON

ACT ONE
Faustus's home, on the occasion of a party for his son

ACT TWO
Variously, Earth, Heaven, and Hell

ACT ONE

■ ■ ■

At rise, we see the portico of FAUSTUS'*s home. Large double doors open onto a room hung with tinsel and streamers, a party scene gotten up as a fantasy.*

FAUSTUS'*s* WIFE *is involved in decoration.* FAUSTUS *enters and looks around. Pause. He holds a sheet of paper in his hand.*

FAUSTUS: It seems a very dream.

WIFE: It is a dream. Delightful, as it is temporary.

FAUSTUS: Temporary.

WIFE: How otherwise?

FAUSTUS: To what do you refer?

WIFE: Have I mistook you?

FAUSTUS: What is it you indict of transience?

WIFE: Of transience—the décor.

FAUSTUS: The décor, of course.

WIFE: Which, you remark, will serve but the day's brief turn . . .

FAUSTUS: . . . of course . . .

WIFE: . . . divert the child, and then . . .

FAUSTUS: How is the boy?

WIFE: He would be thrilled to find you at this unaccustomed hour. What has released you . . . ?

FAUSTUS: . . . and where is Fabian . . . ?

WIFE: I believe he marshals the festivities. I beg your pardon, are you anxious for his news?

FAUSTUS: What news?

WIFE: Today is Friday . . .

FAUSTUS: Yes . . .

WIFE: He generally brings the gazette. Are you cold, Faustus? The day is cold.

FAUSTUS: The chill livens the mind. Life grows in the cold. Does it not?

WIFE: It grows however you should bid.

FAUSTUS: My bidding cannot alter its growth.

WIFE: But it shall affect how I perceive it.

FAUSTUS: I believe I have completed my work. (*Of the paper in his hand*)

WIFE: What . . . ?

FAUSTUS: I believe I have completed it.

WIFE: Your most sanguine of expectations could not put the end sooner than years.

FAUSTUS: So indeed I thought.

WIFE: Then how . . . ?

FAUSTUS: It rests in the rendition of the false. Which, like a bridal veil, could not be lifted by force—solely through devotion. (*He hands her the paper.*)

WIFE: I cannot follow it. The argument's beyond me.

FAUSTUS: Then take me on faith, and pardon me.

WIFE: . . . for what conceivable sin?

FAUSTUS: . . . to leach attention from another's feast. How is the child?

WIFE: He loves you. You repeat yourself.

FAUSTUS: Then you may claim a forfeit.

WIFE: Your soul.

FAUSTUS: Have I not given it?

WIFE: How can you live without your soul?

FAUSTUS: It flourishes without me. While within it was bound by my vice, and vanity, each step for its supposed cultivation only brought it blight. Since consecrated, I observe it to grow strong. Its reproofs are of the most gentle, and its instructions delight.

WIFE: What has it taught you?

FAUSTUS: To yield, to wait, to hope, to believe. In fine, it has taught gratitude.

WIFE: Smile, then, on your faults, as those do who love you. For all must wax and wane.

FAUSTUS: Indeed?

WIFE: Must I quote you the Moon?

FAUSTUS: Oh, simple and good soul, are you not my salvation?

WIFE: As you are mine.

FAUSTUS: Who counted himself honored merely to be your support.

WIFE: Do we not profit, nay, thrive, nay, delight in your wisdom?

FAUSTUS: It is derivative.

WIFE: Must not all wisdom be?

FAUSTUS: Must it?

WIFE: As it derives from God. Our excellence is not in Creation, which is the Lord's, but in our humble wonderment.

FAUSTUS: Which you indict me of?

WIFE: I do.

FAUSTUS: You honor me.

WIFE: I must see to the boy.

FAUSTUS: Stay.

WIFE: He is somewhat overborne by the excitement.

FAUSTUS: Stay. This one moment. Anchor me.

WIFE: This may suffice. (*Hands him a sheet of paper*)

FAUSTUS: What is it?

WIFE: His gift to you.

FAUSTUS: 'Tis his day for gifts.

WIFE: Does he not long to pace you in all things? Who are his god? You fret, he frets; you work, he mimics you, you prepare a gift, so must he . . . and his mind, formed like yours, revolves, ever on the one planetary theme.

FAUSTUS: Whose name is?

WIFE: He pines for you.

FAUSTUS: . . . you give him to understand . . . my work . . .

WIFE: Which names his enemy, but cannot diminish his longing.

FAUSTUS: My sweet son.

WIFE: We have all fretted.

FAUSTUS: Fretted for me?

WIFE: *With* you, say, rather *—with* you—in your seclusion.

FAUSTUS: Yes, I know.

WIFE: Now know the extent. His poem to you. (*She gestures at her sheet of paper.*)

FAUSTUS: (*Reads*)

> *"Heavy heavy the hired man*
> *Weary, how weary the willing hand*
> *One for the Heart, One for the Head*
> *One for the Lad who tarries abed . . ."*
> He stays abed . . . ?

WIFE: . . .'tis but the figure.

FAUSTUS: (*Reads*)

> *"Three swift swallows in the summer sky . . .*
> *Gone in the Twinkling of an eye.*
> *What mystic light, illumes the night*
> *A father's care . . ."*

(*Pause*) This is the Son's love. Full-grown man cannot compass it. But in nostalgia for the infant state . . . that hopeless love of the omnipotent. Sad, savage longing.

WIFE: Sad?

FAUSTUS: Is it not?

WIFE: It turns joyful. Read to the end . . .

FAUSTUS: I recollect, now, for the one half-instant—that brief, child mind, when all good dwelt in self-consuming worship. How might a man deserve it?

WIFE: One may but treasure it. Come to him.

FAUSTUS: In the one moment. My hand to my heart—

WIFE: Then I must go.

FAUSTUS: Again, is he unwell?

WIFE: But overtaxed, anxious for the celebration.

FAUSTUS: Go then, be thou my emissary. Relate my delight at his composition, and offer th' appropriate salutations, as fitting one scribe to his brother upon this festive, so on . . . Bid him allow me to compose myself, after my labor, and I come to him complete.

WIFE: Complete, and abandoned to the festivities.

FAUSTUS: Like a newly convinced addict.

WIFE: And our profound congratulations on the completion of your work. I lack the words . . . might you take them for said?

FAUSTUS: And put so prettily.

WIFE: Where?

FAUSTUS: In your visage—see to the child.

(*She exits.* FAUSTUS *looks at the paper.*)

FAUSTUS: "One for the heart, one for the head, one for the lad who tarries abed . . ." Poor child. His work now complete, he, like his father, is cursed to begin again. For, as much as the work partakes of divine afflautus. To that same extreme one must again tempt, cajole, entreat, and importune the gods. The artist weathercock now ratifying north, now northwest, and we serially nod delight at each fresh revelation. Hush, he is working; hush, he is done. See: our poor petted Sisyphus, watch his labor now devolve from him. Both fame and failure apportioning but self-revulsion. The mind is a mill which can incessant turn, 'til its mere operation focus the stress inward and the stones grind themselves to dust.

(*Enter the* FRIEND)

FRIEND: This is a curious greeting for an anniversary.

FAUSTUS: Fabian.

FRIEND: How is the boy?

FAUSTUS: I was to go to him—I have forgotten. Lord, hear my plea. My sin is great, pardon my self-absorption.

FRIEND: So may we indict any man.

FAUSTUS: And myself the chief malefactor.

FRIEND: Why?

FAUSTUS: The greater the gift the greater the shame in malfeasance, e'en here I sin in pride, how can you stomach me?

FRIEND: Doth not contrition mitigate your pride?

FAUSTUS: It is a counterfeit. Like the rich, I trust to the soft brush of rhetoric, to rasp from me the stench of crime.

FRIEND: Shall nothing cleanse you?

FAUSTUS

FAUSTUS: Mine is the Sin of the Confessional. Of one whose depth of contrition, howe'er impersonated, nay, howe'er felt, may never plumb the depth of his duplicity. I am a fraud. Whose prayer is not thanks, but anxiety: let me be played off, e'er I am discovered.

FRIEND: Not today, not today, good Master, which is a Feast day, when we are bid to drink, to rest, to celebrate.

FAUSTUS: What of philosophy?

FRIEND: And let philosophy succor itself, in whate'er it may consist.

FAUSTUS: While we?

FRIEND: Grope blindly, as your Honor knows, in hope of that good morsel, heady liquor, or compliant wench.

FAUSTUS: Do we then, like the beasts, live solely for repletion?

FRIEND: On the which note might I dare importune you for refreshment?

FAUSTUS: Do I construe you to mean, you find philosophy less than a noble task?

FRIEND: I've seen, these many years, that you enjoy when, at close of day, you have matched this word to that emotion.

FAUSTUS: You find it an unworthy pastime?

FRIEND: Who am I to balk another of his freak? I knew a villain, said he lived to count the stars. Each darkness found him, with his pen and ledger, out of the house, happy as a grig.

FAUSTUS: . . . it pleased him.

FRIEND: He called it his life's work.

FAUSTUS: To number the stars.

FRIEND: So he said. Until that day he wandered out of bounds into a neighbor's copse, and was killed by the gamekeeper.

FAUSTUS: The gamekeeper mistook the fellow's errand.

FRIEND: Oh no, he reckoned it aright.

FAUSTUS: How so?

FRIEND: Each night, my friend took up his ledger and trod out, it was in fact to lie with the gamekeeper's wife.

FAUSTUS: Aha.

FRIEND: *And* daughter.

FAUSTUS: I see your man was a prodigy.

FRIEND: Sir, you don't know the half of it.

FAUSTUS: Which distinguishes me from the gamekeeper's wife.

FRIEND: . . . *and* daughter . . .

FAUSTUS: . . . as you said.

FRIEND: . . . *and* son, for all we know.

FAUSTUS: . . . so much is hidden from us . . . (*Pause*) You balk me of my prerogative melancholy.

FRIEND: You have enrolled me as your foil. Permit me my turn. Again, might you supply a drink, to a traveler, come from the cold unfeeling world?

FAUSTUS: Ah, have you brought the journal?

FRIEND: The journal, no.

FAUSTUS: You have not?

FRIEND: But is it Friday?

FAUSTUS: Returned, with its noted regularity.

FRIEND: I do not have the journal, no.

FAUSTUS: Oh, my friend, you are damned to Hell. Heaven must shun you, as you use its gifts so ill.

FRIEND: What gift?

FAUSTUS: Mendacity. Give me the gazette.

FRIEND: I do not have it.

FAUSTUS: Give it in any case.

FRIEND: I would not vex you on this party day.

FAUSTUS: I warrant you I shall survive what your reluctance indicates as their displeasure.

FRIEND: They have, we must note, historically praised you.

FAUSTUS: They praise me, as they praise the mother of the bride, to mask their own concupiscence. What is their praise, they are, as dolt schoolchildren bent over their sums, they round their inclusivities, into the most proximate low error. Their censure and applause are one. But th' extorted approbation of the mob. Crowds who cry up this slaughterer, that thief as great? Give me sufficient ink and paper, I'll make a dog's bone beloved of the world.

FRIEND: Do you shun fame?

FAUSTUS: I accept it. I pursue knowledge.

FRIEND: Would you then publish your work anonymously?

FAUSTUS: Discovered, I confess. Am I a libertine? A thief? A murderer? I covet fame. And, like the criminal I plead first, what have I done, and next, who suffered? Yes. I would have fame. For my works, and fame surpassing them, til Faustus's renown shines free of accomplishment. Read me the journal.

FRIEND: Read it to you?

FAUSTUS: The honest man—must in good modesty avert his gaze. It is a disgraceful proclivity. The journals.

FRIEND: To write them?

FAUSTUS: To *read* them. To write them is a crime against nature. What do they say of me?

FRIEND: Pray, delay it past this festive time. How is the boy?

FAUSTUS: He has a cold upon the chest. Read the report to me.

FRIEND: (*Takes out a newspaper and reads*) . . . that . . .

FAUSTUS: . . . please . . .

FRIEND: . . . my eyes as you know are weak.

FAUSTUS: . . . supply the lack with concentration.

FRIEND: "Our celebrated polymath, our local champion . . ."

FAUSTUS: Now we enlarge the epigram: even a dead pig finds a truffle. Read on . . .

FRIEND: "Faustus: our premier: physician, philosopher, savant-scientist . . ."

FAUSTUS: A linguistic supererogation . . .

FRIEND: ". . . having labored for," et cetera . . .

FAUSTUS: . . . I shall respond to them.

FRIEND: "Proceeds, our sources inform us . . ."

FAUSTUS: . . . who might these sources be?

FRIEND: Friends of yourself, and friends of knowledge?

FAUSTUS: Ah yes, the hopeful constituency of the seekers-after-light, the talented who worship genius, the mediocre, who doubt its existence. Whom do I lack?

FRIEND: The Average Man. You omit that creature.

FAUSTUS: Has he, then, heard of me?

FRIEND: Does he not read the journal?

FAUSTUS: As the mariner rivets his gaze to the lighthouse.

FRIEND: What must he make of you—Faustus?

FAUSTUS: Please . . . ?

FRIEND: In truth, accomplished, celebrated, wealthy, loved
. . . how may he compass it? This average man?

FAUSTUS: How can we know? Our Biblia Sacra treats not
of him, but of ourself. Say on . . .

FRIEND: Are you immune?

FAUSTUS: Let's make the trial. (*Pause*)

FRIEND: ". . . that we have tired of the oft-reiterated phrase
that we may expect, momentarily, the completion of
the long awaited . . ." I had rather not continue.

FAUSTUS: Does it turn combative? (*Pause*) Does it suggest
I have been o'erpraised? And that a new, unsenti-
mental day, judge between merit and nostalgia?
Does it suggest "brief Comet, in the firmament, and
long-deferred hope of its return . . ."?

FRIEND: Are you, then, clairvoyant, to read the hidden page?

FAUSTUS: They are a newspaper. How may continued praise be news? It may not. Read on, though I could have writ it.

FRIEND: (*Reads*) ". . . as an uncontracted burden, upon our intellectual establishment; the tax of continued praise for this juvenilia, of long-deferred hope for completion of a notional magnum opus. The repeated postponement of which must call to doubt its very existence . . . Our praise of Faustus . . ."

FAUSTUS: I have completed my work.

FRIEND: Say again.

FAUSTUS: I have completed it.

FRIEND: When?

FAUSTUS: (*Passing him the paper*) Smudge the fresh ink with your finger, and add your mark to the colophon.

FRIEND: Would it were so . . .

FAUSTUS: You'd wish it?

FRIEND: You speak from Parnassus, to him the gods delight to ignore. Will you license me, Faustus, to express my deep honor, and my profound sense of occasion?

FAUSTUS: Equally, my friend, who have supported me. For in my doubt I treasured your belief.

FRIEND: You doubted, Faustus . . . ?

FAUSTUS: How could I but doubt? Who played with this or that prideful manipulation. Til I found not the piece I sought, but an inversion of the paradigm. I have been a fool occupied with toys. I have misused the gifts vouchsafed to me.

FRIEND: How possibly?

FAUSTUS: Through the very conjectural disclaimers of worth, each calculated or to increase my fame, or to propitiate nemesis. You wish to ruin a man, praise him for his self-known hypocrisies. For gold's ever fresh-minted in delight, but its worth is untied to the form, but part of the earth's primal store. (*Pause*) In fine, praise God, and let them say this of me: He was rewarded for his brute persistence. Not for an act but for a submission.

FRIEND: A submission?

FAUSTUS: For is not the answer constantly before us . . .

FRIEND: And your work treats of the Answer?

FAUSTUS: . . . as you say.

FRIEND: And may you capsulate it?

FAUSTUS: Read . . . Read. Here: it is a mathematic formula. That is all. It is a numeric reduction.

FRIEND: (*Takes the paper*) Surely its study requires diligence.

FAUSTUS: Indeed.

FRIEND: The computation is abstruse, the equation beyond my mathematic skills.

FAUSTUS: Here is the coda . . .

FRIEND: How shall I grasp it absent the foundation?

FAUSTUS: Attend:

(*The* WIFE *enters.*)

WIFE: Fabian.

FRIEND: My dear, I understand that I am doubly to felicitate you.

WIFE: Fabian, welcome. Faustus . . .

FAUSTUS: In the one moment . . . will it hold?

WIFE: For the one moment, of course . . .

FRIEND: (*To* WIFE) Will you hear my speech? I shall extemporize th' addition . . .

WIFE: With thanks, but presently, I must see to the boy. (*She exits.*)

FRIEND: Is he unwell?

FAUSTUS: Children, like the Mass, act in the responsive state, they quaver to the air, the moon, a drop in the glass, the helictic motion of the spheres. How could he otherwise than resonate at my discovery? See, now the very humors in the sway of periodic power.

FRIEND: Of periodic Power.

FAUSTUS: (*Of his manuscript page*) See, see here. Read:

FRIEND: It is beyond me.

FAUSTUS: Read the preamble. See. That Number. That all is reducible to periodicity. To cipher, to a formula, expressed in number; and that number signifies not quantity . . . not quantity. But a progression. (*Pause*)

FRIEND: . . . I am at a loss, my friend.

FAUSTUS: No—stay—I shall parcel it slowly.

FRIEND: Fit your description to my limits.

FAUSTUS: Consider the boy.

FRIEND: For which my felicitations.

FAUSTUS: Many thanks. Now see him age.

FRIEND: Which, may God in his beneficence permit.

FAUSTUS: Amen, with all my heart. Now we admit him as a youth, surprised, by first love, later by betrothal, marriage, and conception. Each, to his eye, a personal, nay idiosyncratic ebullition. Yet, from our remove, inevitable, universal.

FRIEND: Thus?

FAUSTUS: And thus predictable. There is a generalized periodicity . . . Which, once revealed's encountered everywhere. I instance: the recurrence of drought, famine, fire, and, by extension, those eruptions we, untutored, understand, as acts of will: war, civic growth, invention, and decay . . . Had one sufficient remove, one could plot the concordance.

FRIEND: Of?

FAUSTUS: Of acts of nature, and supposed acts of will. In short, of human movement. (*Pause*) There is a consonance. It is a code. It is called periodicity. It is the secret engine of the world.

FRIEND: You here profess to comprehend it?

FAUSTUS: Read. (*Pause*)

FRIEND: Is it not blasphemy?

FAUSTUS: Blasphemy and prayer are one. Both assert the existence of a superior power. The first, however, with conviction.

FRIEND: But should one stray too far . . . ?

FAUSTUS: How might one stray too far?

FRIEND: Permit me, if I may, to counsel respect for the jocular proclivities we know to be the gods. Were it not better to refrain? Do not tempt fate.

FAUSTUS: What is my charge but to tempt fate? Each time I commence and each conclude?

FRIEND: Until?

FAUSTUS: Until God recoil at the impertinence? (*Pause*) He bids the farmer find delight in the pristine, the entrepreneur in the ruined, the philosopher in the occluded. As sentries on the battlement, shall we not be drawn to the edge?

FRIEND: And cautioned to refrain.

FAUSTUS: Yet incited to leap.

FRIEND: By?

FAUSTUS: An echo of forgotten power, as in the life of birds.

FRIEND: Do we descend from birds? Say angels.

FAUSTUS: Both, you remark, can fly.

FRIEND: You frighten me.

FAUSTUS: Is it not my duty? Hand me the journal—I will respond to them.

FRIEND: Would I were more intelligent, or to dispute or second your conclusions.

FAUSTUS: Each trade must bear its occupation mark. The ploughman's gnarled hands, the blacksmith's seared forearm.

FRIEND: And the philosopher?

FAUSTUS: A certain melancholy—the dual conviction of futility and prescience. A cook with but two spices, ever attempting to amend with one, his error with the other. (*Pause*) Enough. I have transgressed, not the prerogatives of the gods, but the more comprehensible strictures of good manners. Today's the boy's.

FRIEND: Indeed.

FAUSTUS: He wrote to me.

FRIEND: He did?

FAUSTUS: A poem. (FAUSTUS *hands the poem to his* FRIEND.)

(*The* FRIEND *reads the poem.*)

FRIEND: "What mystic light illumes the night. A father's care . . ." This is a sign of grace.

FAUSTUS: Is that a scientific term?

FRIEND: Never a cynic but concealed acolyte *in potentia*.

FAUSTUS: And what brave man divulged the theory?

FRIEND: You did.

FAUSTUS: Your learning does you credit. "A father's care." Perhaps it is grace.

FRIEND: What a concession.

FAUSTUS: Yes, why should I be chosen?

FRIEND: All are chosen.

FAUSTUS: All are chosen? Then what possible meaning has the term?

FRIEND: We are all subject to God's grace.

FAUSTUS: Bless me, he treads damn near the theological.

FRIEND: You say you seek a greater power.

FAUSTUS: A greater power than *that*, certainly.

FRIEND: Than what?

FAUSTUS: Than *religion*.

FRIEND: There is no greater power.

FAUSTUS: Then why does one find, under its aegis, nay, in its name, more progressed misery, murder, and starvation than exists in an unbeneficed state of nature? Answer me that and go free.

FRIEND: Many find it a source of strength.

FAUSTUS: The leaf of the camomile, parboiled in water, conduces to calm. And yet I do not worship it.

FRIEND: You spoke of a greater power—

FAUSTUS: I spoke of *number*.

FRIEND: Number.

FAUSTUS: Yes. Not religion, which to the scientific mind cannot be quantified.

FRIEND: Is it, then, worthless?

FAUSTUS: To the scientist.

FRIEND: Then how comes religion to cleanse?

FAUSTUS: A candle gains in power as we still warring illumination. Were we to flood the room with light, the object of our interest, of our longing, of our worship is forgot. For it is nothing. (*Pause*)

FRIEND: It is salvation.

FAUSTUS: Then seek it. As each man seeks himself, in all things. This is the law of life.

FRIEND: I understand, of course, your enthusiasm.

FAUSTUS: . . . your mitigating clause?

FRIEND: I simply suggest reserve of speech.

FAUSTUS: Speech cannot alter the unfolding of the natural order.

FRIEND: And what of miracle?

FAUSTUS: Instance it—

FRIEND: Many invoke Salvation.

FAUSTUS: And many believe in war, yet remark that they do not fight.

FRIEND: But:

FAUSTUS: Say on.

FRIEND: To impugn. The power of the Church to save . . .

FAUSTUS: Proclaimed by whom but man?

FRIEND: Christ's word is divine.

FAUSTUS: Proclaimed . . . ?

FRIEND: By the Council of Nicaea.

FAUSTUS: Who, if I do not err, were men.

FRIEND: But this is heresy.

FAUSTUS: Greater than theirs? (*Pause*) Greater than theirs?

FRIEND: I do believe it.

FAUSTUS: This too is an equation. There are but two paths by which men may thrive: the direct pursuit of power, and the propitiation of its possessors.

FRIEND: But some do good.

FAUSTUS: Yes?

FRIEND: Do you grant it?

FAUSTUS: If it amuses you.

(FAUSTUS's WIFE *enters.*)

WIFE: Faustus.

FAUSTUS: One moment. (*Pause*) Do I vex you? Do I confound? All of your adjurations, to recant, are but reminders to speak hypocritically, as all men speak. (*Pause*) You fear the impending limit of the circumscribed. You cling to: tradition, reason, custom, common sense, an intelligent submission. And I ask: to what?

FRIEND: Then what is not to be despised?

WIFE: Our love for a child, which seeks nothing for itself.

FAUSTUS: Save immortality.

WIFE: I was bid announce your arrival. We take you at your word—he waits for you. I do not mean to vex you in your happy completion . . .

FAUSTUS: No, no. The fault is mine. (*She exits.*) Well, then, you see, the poor philosopher, jerked from his native element of disputation, struggles on the bank. I must go.

FRIEND: But is there no excellence?

FAUSTUS: Yes. I have troubled you.

FRIEND: Is all but *number*? I understand you to speak hyperbolically . . .

FAUSTUS: I do not.

FRIEND: But does naught exist, absent your formula?

FAUSTUS: Else, of what worth the equation?

FRIEND: But, the ineffable: hope, courage . . .

FAUSTUS: Show it to me.

FRIEND: In the military.

FAUSTUS: They hone the scabbard while the saber rusts. Bravo the generals.

FRIEND: Say in the private soldier?

FAUSTUS: He fights from rage, fear, or shame—who does not?

FRIEND: In the devotion of the pedagogue.

FAUSTUS: To drill the young to say five things about seven books.

FRIEND: Say, in the law, in jurisprudence.

FAUSTUS: Many remark justice is blind; pity those in her sway, shocked to discover she is also deaf.

FRIEND: Then in the service of the State.

FAUSTUS: In what consists the State? A salubrity of climate or geography, o'erlaid by the posturings of the suborned; unwashed cupidity, license for murder . . . Oh, if I were king.

FRIEND: Be still, they might elect you.

FAUSTUS: Heaven forfend.

FRIEND: And, e'en a king's power is circumscribed.

FAUSTUS: As whose is not.

FRIEND: God's, people say.

FAUSTUS: Then how explain human suffering?

FRIEND: His power is limitless to do. Ours is curtailed to understand.

FAUSTUS: A good, traditional response.

(*The* MAGUS *appears, with a flourish of drums. He carries a valise marked with a devil's head.*)

FAUSTUS: Selah. Who have we here? Is it the Devil . . . Sir, are you the Devil?

MAGUS: His counterfeit, my lord, upon the earth.

WIFE: (*Drawn by the sound*) Faustus, who has engaged the entertainer?

FAUSTUS: Right welcome. Are we not told, of periodic riots of inversion, where we find license to resolve our various superfluities? Heathen societies knew it as orgy, we, their ailing, decadent descendants call it holiday. Here is the last pagan survival welcome, sir—what do you bring?

MAGUS: Signor, we bring a carnival.

FAUSTUS: Bravo.

WIFE: I fear the boy unequal to the entertainment.

FAUSTUS: Then I shall bear the shock. (*The* WIFE *retires.*)
Dare we hope that you come to subvert the natural
order?

MAGUS: As you may judge. Vouchsafe the moment for our
preparation, and we shall reveal the occult, and set
at defiance: time, space, and logic, law, and decorum.

FAUSTUS: Proceed—proceed, sir, are we not yours?

(The MAGUS *performs a magical flourish, and then intones:*)

MAGUS:

Ecco
The carnival
Wherein, all rights reversed,
We abjure hypocrisy
O blessed traveler,
Who quits his burden as if ne'er to
Reassume it
Cast from you care, disport as before th' invention
of remorse
The timid call themselves philosophers
The bolder libertines
Each, however, once subsumed, becomes the acolyte.
The disparate revealed as one, the whole as mosaic
As we shatter the oppressive unities til space,
matter, thought and life itself are called by the one
name
Jubio!

(*The* MAGUS *does a magical trick.*)

FAUSTUS: Oh, sir. Need we fear?

MAGUS: Naught but the mysteries . . .

(FAUSTUS *applauds.*)

FAUSTUS: All reverence to the lord of misrule. Honor, of course, to the Creator, but to the inverter, ten thousand times more. Poor ignorant folk, here below, we've glimpsed the world the wrong way, round, now may we stare, delighted at the back of the tapestry. Or have we gazed, all our lives, at its inversion? (*To* MAGUS) What do you say?

MAGUS: I have prayed for a man to understand me.

FAUSTUS: Am I that man?

MAGUS: From your speech, sir, I'd have took you for one of the confraternity.

FAUSTUS: No, I am but a poor projector. Yours is the core of accomplishment.

MAGUS: The core, sir?

FAUSTUS: Are we not told, the jesters of a wiser day, made all whole in shaking a skull at their masters? Have you heard that tale?

MAGUS: I have, but cannot credit it.

FAUSTUS: Nor I, for where, among the great, do we find self-depreciation? (FAUSTUS *takes up the gazette.*) Nor should one feel the need, when these exist, detractors by profession—eunuch compilers, swine... (*Reads*) "Our petted savant ... fat on the leavings of a prior fame." ... Another trick, sir, loose me a diverting marvel.

FRIEND: Shall we not await the child?

FAUSTUS: Do not subvert the flow of the performance. Charm me, from the world.

MAGUS: I can but conjure, sir, as I am skilled, which extends but to the distraction of the uninformed...

FRIEND: Behold another of your confraternity: (*Of the paper*) Continue.

MAGUS: Bid me.

FAUSTUS: (*Of the newspaper*) Make this foul indictment disappear.

MAGUS: (*Takes the newspaper, and, with a flourish, disappears it*) *Ecco*. It vanishes.

FAUSTUS: No!

MAGUS: Sir, to the contrary.

FAUSTUS: Oh, bravo.

MAGUS: I did not o'erextend my brief . . . ?

FAUSTUS: Indeed you did. Well done and excellently improvised. My hand.

MAGUS: Most honored.

FAUSTUS: To have fooled the philosopher.

MAGUS: One finds, in my profession, sir, the greater the intellect, the more ease in its misdirection.

FAUSTUS: One finds the same in mine. Oh, well done. To have shrunk that canker. It lacks but the one dimension, your trick.

MAGUS: . . . servant, sir.

FAUSTUS: Cleanse it from memory.

(*Pause*)

MAGUS: Give me but time.

FAUSTUS: Bravo. Bravo, sir. Well said.

(*The* WIFE *again appears.*)

FAUSTUS: . . . one moment. Here's a worthy adversary, which is to say, companion . . . godlike, makes matter dissipate, the savant smile with content . . .

(*The* FRIEND *comes over to* FAUSTUS *and whispers to him.*)

FAUSTUS: Yes, aid her. With thanks.

(*The two exit, leaving* FAUSTUS *and the* MAGUS.)

FAUSTUS: With the one word. You win me to your cause, I abjure philosophy and embrace prestidigitation. Where do we part? Each utters a meaningless phrase to allow the mass to ascribe to them a power not their own. In your case, thaumaturgy, in mine, wisdom. Another effect. (*The* MAGUS *takes out a large silk.*) No—improvise . . .

MAGUS: Direct me.

FAUSTUS: Cure me my autumn cold.

MAGUS: Are you unwell?

FAUSTUS: But with the change of season.

MAGUS: Take to your bed, and meditate upon a yellow light.

FAUSTUS: Shall I be thus cured?

MAGUS: Within the quarter hour. But you in no event must allow your mind freedom from this curative fluorescence. One tenth, one twentieth second of impertinence, the cure is null. And the disease shall worsen.

FAUSTUS: Unto death?

MAGUS: Unless your will be of the strongest, I would forgo the test.

FAUSTUS: Physician-philosopher. May we suppose your powers have no end?

MAGUS: Try me.

FAUSTUS: What is the engine of the world?

MAGUS: The engine of the world's regret.

FAUSTUS: Then, as you are a magus, proof me from it.

MAGUS: Here is a sovereign talisman against regret: never do that which might engender it.

FAUSTUS: Oh, best of magicians. Are you then skilled to banish all disruption?

MAGUS: Sir, on the instant.

(*The* MAGUS *prepares to perform a magical pass.*)

(*The* WIFE *enters.*)

MAGUS: Watch here.

WIFE: Faustus.

FAUSTUS: Of course. Sir: with my apologies, to stunt your effect.

MAGUS: Your servant.

FAUSTUS: And here take my leave—but with the one question.

MAGUS: Please . . .

FAUSTUS: Where is the newspaper?

MAGUS: Sir, it is gone.

FAUSTUS: Can matter be annihilated?

MAGUS: Alas.

FAUSTUS: No, but reveal me the trick.

MAGUS: My revelation could not bring delight.

FAUSTUS: May I not judge?

MAGUS: In my profession, as in yours, that given free must be despised.

FAUSTUS: Indeed?

MAGUS: It is the one sure, certain law of life.

FAUSTUS: Name me your forfeit.

MAGUS: Your respect, for I am asked to do that which can but cause disillusion.

FAUSTUS: You have my respect. I swear it.

MAGUS: (*The* MAGUS *magically produces the newspaper.*) *Ecco*:

(FAUSTUS *takes the newspaper.*)

FAUSTUS: But this is not the gazette. The page is blank . . .

WIFE: The child is unwell.

FAUSTUS: He is but overset.

WIFE: Yes.

FRIEND: Must we annul the entertainment?

WIFE: Come with me now, Faustus. Enough.

FAUSTUS: One moment, while I close with the jester. (*To* FRIEND) Would you fetch my purse?

FRIEND: (*As he hands* FAUSTUS *a purse*) Here is mine.

FAUSTUS: (*As he hands a sheet of paper to his* FRIEND) Thank you, please, and be so good as to return this page to my manuscript. You remark, it is the final page . . .

FRIEND: . . . great honor.

FAUSTUS: Go with my wife. Do not fret for the child. Surfeit must be released. Heavy air weighs on the lungs, the storms discharge it.

(*The* FRIEND *exits.*)

FAUSTUS: (*To the* MAGUS) Maestro, my pardon. Take this (*Of the purse*), and with my thanks, I would not for the world release you, but as you perceive . . .

MAGUS: Servant, sir.

FAUSTUS: I pray but for the restoration of the gazette.

MAGUS: I beg your pardon?

FAUSTUS: Where is the journal?

MAGUS: Sir, it is vanished.

FAUSTUS: Quite. But where? Shall I turn my back?

MAGUS: Sir, I have made the incantation, and the component atoms of the subject article . . .

FAUSTUS: Indeed, then, I must class myself with those who, doubtless, importune you to reveal the secrets of your worthy craft.

MAGUS: Would you, again, sir, trade delight for disillusionment . . . ?

FAUSTUS: I do not seek delight, but restoration. I require the journal.

MAGUS: Sir, I am at a stand.

FAUSTUS: Sir: did you have me swear? Did you tax me to swear?

MAGUS: I do not know, how, in faith, I may unclothe my craft.

FAUSTUS: Did you not have me mime a ceremony, to do just that?

MAGUS: Indeed, it was but to augment th' effect . . . 'tis not for the uninitiated . . .

FAUSTUS: Oh. Do I transgress a magical divide? Do I encroach upon the netherworld . . . ? Shall I avert my unschooled gaze lest it be seared by the mysteries . . . ? Poor uninitiate, to wander, sightless in the sacred grove. Do I offend? I beg pardon; but have I not contracted for your energy? And now have you, as comes to any artist, o'er reached yourself? Must you renounce your excellence, and crawl to kennel like a beaten dog, your poor trick revealed? How unlike the omnipotent priest you impersonate. (*Pause*) Have you not been paid? Why do you hesitate?

MAGUS: I held, sir, but the one moment to compose my thought. For onlookers, discovering an illusion, fall into self-contempt, and, indeed, oft, to anger. I strove but for a happy way to effect the restoration. I assure you I intended no disrespect. (*Of purse*) You have over-rewarded me, who did not, in fact, perform. If I, in my search for a graceful exit, caused offense, I humbly beg your pardon. Please guard this pledge of my sincerity. (*The* MAGUS *restores the purse to* FAUSTUS.) The journal may be found beneath your feet.

(*The* MAGUS *begins to exit.*)

FAUSTUS: Wait, friend, wait, I beg you hear me, though, indeed, I have no merit to plead. I have, I second you, traduced whatever claim upon your graciousness. And I have mocked you. In giddy self-absorption. I have no excuse, and can but beg your pardon.

MAGUS: I do not comprehend you, sir.

FAUSTUS: Indeed you do, oh, stay, and forgive me. Wait, while I delineate it: We had engaged you. To perform, who bought your time, and owe you, in return, attention . . .

MAGUS: Not were my play to fail . . .

FAUSTUS: In any case, civility. From which we may not be exempted. I am in breach. And plead, not as your contractor, but as one man to his like, you feign a god, and I a philosopher. Forgive me. Who most completely regrets his offense.

MAGUS: (*Pause*) It were above me to forgive you.

FAUSTUS: Oh no, naught but our parity wipes the slate clean.

MAGUS: None but you has the power to suggest it.

FAUSTUS: Must that debar me from my suit?

MAGUS: You plead your right to waive preferment.

FAUSTUS: I do.

MAGUS: And yet, I cannot waive my subordination.

FAUSTUS: Oh, my friend. Which makes my gaffe the less excusable. I am ashamed of my intemperate speech and offer my sincere apology. (*Pause*)

MAGUS: You entice me to my better self.

FAUSTUS: I ask your pardon.

MAGUS: Were I to forward but its simulacrum?

FAUSTUS: Come, sir, finally, let us be friends. Shall we not
be friends? Mired together, in this what shall we
say . . . ? *Aid* me . . . in . . . ?

MAGUS: In a dark wood.

FAUSTUS: In this underworld. Which you and I know as
the world's nickname. Two philosophers, two show-
men, seeking to astound, are we not?

MAGUS: You, sir, through your perception, I through
trickery . . .

FAUSTUS: Each though, libel to frightened slander. Do I tax
the conceit? My yokemate, as we pull the world on?

MAGUS: You o'er flatter me . . .

FAUSTUS: As we: reason and folly, two paired oxen, wrestle
the wagon of the world . . . ah, you smile, and now,
encouraged by your approbation, having tapped its
depth shall I now try its elasticity? Where did I leave
my burden?

MAGUS: In a dark wood . . .

FAUSTUS: In the dark wood, yes, our rough conveyance, fast in the mire, no purchase, night coming on . . .

MAGUS: You have neglected the storm.

FAUSTUS: I stipulate it per tradition. And the cart, aid me, my friend.

MAGUS: Upon whose side we daub the name Humanity . . .

FAUSTUS: . . . oh, precious perishable cargo . . . left to the strength . . .

MAGUS: Abandoned to the faltering strength . . .

FAUSTUS: Of its mismatched beasts of travail: philosophy and Magic . . . its castrated fattened cattle: Amuse me from this Wood, oh, Magus. From this dark wood. From loneliness, my brother. Oh, poor souls—who would begrudge us our self-pity—alone empowered, are we not?

MAGUS: Are we, sir?

FAUSTUS: Possessors of that Secret Knowledge. And unable to discharge the burden.

MAGUS: To the which end, the paired oxen must pull together.

FAUSTUS: There you are, my friend. A meeting in the dark wood. For it doth turn a burden, now and then . . .

MAGUS: In any pursuit . . .

FAUSTUS: I would imagine, the uncertainty, the need to please . . .

MAGUS: Recurring, periodic self-doubt, sir, as we, increasing, master the few tricks, and, daily, doubt their worth.

FAUSTUS: You speak, sir, for the company. (*Pause*)

MAGUS: Who drives your figure?

FAUSTUS: Eh?

MAGUS: You speak of the oxen, and their cart . . . who is it directs them?

FAUSTUS: Ah, yes, whom may we say? Who is the goad?

MAGUS: Perhaps, the family . . .

FAUSTUS: The family.

MAGUS: Perhaps one toils for their comfort, their safety and education.

FAUSTUS: Perhaps.

MAGUS: Is it not so?

FAUSTUS: Though, oft in our secret selves, we indict them, do we not?

MAGUS: Indict them, you say, sir?

FAUSTUS: For their claim upon us.

MAGUS: A legitimate claim.

FAUSTUS: How much the more oppressive?

MAGUS: When is a man content?

FAUSTUS: I ask you. When may one be content? When work, and admiration, family, fame, nay, and *posterity* continually importune for acknowledgment. What poor conflicted souls. Who falsely name their pursuit "liberty."

MAGUS: What is its secret name? (*Pause*)

FAUSTUS: Revenge. Those with whom I contend, are phantoms. Those I instruct fools, or e'er either to avoid, or e'er applaud the obvious. I fear failure, I sicken of success, my sinews set in the mold in which work has stiffened them. I am unfitted even to unbend. I beg thee, brother, purge my soul of its self-content, show me the upper world, and I will follow. Poor, petted Faustus implores thee.

MAGUS: I scarce know how to take you, sir.

FAUSTUS: No, no, induct me. Blister my flesh upon the candle, cause me to proffer oaths.

MAGUS: What oaths?

FAUSTUS: Whate'er is traditional . . .

(*Offstage cries are heard.*)

MAGUS: The child cries.

FAUSTUS: Its cries will cease. Shrive me. Bid me renounce th' immaterial world. I regret my preferment and beg for the chance to begin anew.

MAGUS: Ah: That is a plea I recognize.

FAUSTUS: Then pity me. Ultimate physician.

MAGUS: Another bears that name.

FAUSTUS: Perhaps you are his servant?

MAGUS: All are within his thrall.

FAUSTUS: Indeed?

MAGUS: Is there not said to be salvation?

FAUSTUS: Who returns to demonstrate it? (*Pause*) What powers shall we importune?

MAGUS: I cede to you the choice.

FAUSTUS: Teach me a trick.

MAGUS: I shall reveal a trick, in fact, the greatest of illusions: (*The* MAGUS *prepares to perform a magical flourish.*)

(*The* FRIEND *appears.*)

FRIEND: Faustus.

MAGUS: . . . Behold.

FRIEND: Your wife sends to summon you.

FAUSTUS: It is the child.

FRIEND: It is.

MAGUS: May all its trials be transient.

FAUSTUS: It cries from excitement. It cries for a bruise at play. Its cries are sweet, for it may be comforted.

FRIEND: Your wife bids you attend immediately. (*Pause*) Faustus.

FAUSTUS: (*To the* MAGUS) Sir, I would not for the world, again, offend you. But, as you see. Sadly, as you see.

MAGUS: Of course.

FAUSTUS: (*To the* FRIEND) I come on the instant. (*The* FRIEND *exits. To the* MAGUS) My thanks, sir, from the heart, for your companionship. I forestall, until that day, the renewed delight of our continued brotherhood.

MAGUS: You asked to be taught a trick.

FAUSTUS: I must plead a postponement.

MAGUS: E'en to discover the most complete effect?

FAUSTUS: I do not doubt your skill. Howe'er, my duties abrogate even your power, O Magus, to transfix me. Servant, sir.

(FAUSTUS *starts to depart.*)

MAGUS: Your manuscript contains an error.

FAUSTUS: (*Pause*) What?

MAGUS: As I have said.

FAUSTUS: Ah. Yes. Well done. My manuscript. An overheard exchange prompts an improvisation. A misplaced punctuation mark, an orthographic fault.

MAGUS: It hides an error, which, to posterity serves to nullify the work entire.

FAUSTUS: Have you then seen the future?

MAGUS: It is one with the past.

FAUSTUS: Absent the provoking generalities.

MAGUS: Do you challenge me?

FAUSTUS: I do. What do you know of my philosophy?

MAGUS: 'Tis said you are like Adam, before whom were brought all God's creation, and whate'er he chose to call them, so they were called. And now you are complete. Your long years journey summarized in mathematical perfection.

FAUSTUS: You speak of my new work?

MAGUS: I do.

FAUSTUS: I penned the last page but this afternoon.

MAGUS: You wish me to quote it to you.

FAUSTUS: I do.

MAGUS: "Wherein we find that number . . ."

FAUSTUS: No . . .

MAGUS: Indeed, "is not, and signifies not a quantity, but a progression." Shall I continue? Shall I quote the formula?

FRIEND: (*Entering*) Faustus.

FAUSTUS: Stop. He has purloined the manuscript.

FRIEND: Faustus, the child cries . . .

FAUSTUS: Are you a thief?

MAGUS: I am not.

FAUSTUS: Then how have you divined my thesis's burden?

MAGUS: I cannot debase my trade to the uninitiated.

FAUSTUS: Is it then, mere manipulation?

MAGUS: That is the charge I must withhold.

FAUSTUS: Who bids you? Are you a *spy*?

MAGUS: I assure you I am not.

FAUSTUS: Are you a telepath, sir, no, then I say you are a thief . . .

FRIEND: Faustus . . .

FAUSTUS: ... one moment. (*The* FRIEND *exits.*) Ah, well done. I had insulted you, and wronged your craft. And though we kissed rings must you not have your revenge. And, now, you have had your revenge ... Now you have bested me. Now we may cry quits. Now. You quote my conclusions in my actual language. This is an effect which ...

MAGUS: But if it is not an effect ...

FAUSTUS: You vex me with fooling, sir. Howe'er you call it, effect, illusion, nay, a miracle: Induct me, but for the one circumstance. I will not reveal your art. I plead not from mere curiosity, but from material concern. For the security of my work, of my manuscript ...

MAGUS: But what if the manuscript ... were to contain a fault.

FAUSTUS: ... please.

MAGUS: Grant it hypothetically.

FAUSTUS: Is that your precondition?

MAGUS: What if your manuscript contained a disqualificatory error? (*Pause*)

FAUSTUS: I would amend it.

MAGUS: And if to do so were to unpick its essential
fiber . . . (*Pause*) To unsay the Work entire . . . ?

FAUSTUS: I cannot imagine such a fault.

MAGUS: But if such were revealed to you . . . a fault which
were, to all succeeding age, to cast your work as a
by-word, and a jest.

FAUSTUS: Instance an example of such error.

MAGUS: If it were stolen from another. (*Pause*)

FAUSTUS: But it is not.

MAGUS: But if it were. That would, of course, set it as an
example of that error which might not be put aright.

FAUSTUS: Deservedly.

MAGUS: If it were purloined.

FAUSTUS: Yes.

MAGUS: In whole or part.

FAUSTUS: As I have said. Thus?

MAGUS: You asked me to instance a category of error. I
have done so.

FAUSTUS: Yes, there's your small casuistic victory. I grant the category. My work, however, is unblemished.

MAGUS: So you say.

FAUSTUS: I do.

MAGUS: But would you swear an oath?

FAUSTUS: I do not follow you, sir.

MAGUS: Indeed you do, but cannot overtake me . . . You press me to reveal the occult. To protect, as you say, the sanctity of your creation, you ask me to unclothe my own. I reply: swear it is yours entire.

FAUSTUS: It is.

MAGUS: Upon your family. (*Pause*) And yet you will not assert it.

FAUSTUS: The thoughtful hesitate to take an oath.

MAGUS: The thoughtful.

FAUSTUS: It is from a sense of probity.

MAGUS: Not from fear . . . ?

FAUSTUS: I think not.

MAGUS: As who would say "I swear on my life," or "on my children's life" . . .

FAUSTUS: But who would proffer such an oath?

MAGUS: What is the risk?

FAUSTUS: Not risk, but impropriety. As who would sully the name of his wife, say, in a tavern; of his children, in the street. These practices are private, not to be profanely uttered.

MAGUS: And yet we swear to God, and account it a jest.

FAUSTUS: With respect, this is a disquisition not on the notional Dark Forces, but on the vagaries of language.

MAGUS: Ah, language is all.

FAUSTUS: The cries of birds may communicate some little-more-than-instinct, one to the next, but are to the higher order, nothing more than song. As must our plaintive imprecations be to those chimerical Powers above.

MAGUS: And yet we hesitate before them.

FAUSTUS: Again, what does it signify?

MAGUS: That is my question, sir, to you.

FAUSTUS: I swear the work is mine.

MAGUS: Upon your family.

FAUSTUS: Were I proved in default.

MAGUS: . . . by whom?

FAUSTUS: I swear the work is of my invention complete, entire.

MAGUS: Upon the lives of your wife and child.

FAUSTUS: Tell how you knew of my formula.

MAGUS: I will not reveal myself to one unbound. Will you swear? (*Pause*) Will you swear?

(*Pause*)

FAUSTUS: I will.

MAGUS: Upon the dirk. (*He draws the dirk and holds it in front of* FAUSTUS.) Grasp it.

(FAUSTUS *takes the dirk.*)

FAUSTUS: I swear upon the lives of my wife and child. The manuscript is mine entire. Are you content? Am I now sworn?

MAGUS: You are.

FAUSTUS: Then divulge to me how you came to know of my work's conclusion.

MAGUS: I overheard your shortsighted friend, muttering the phrases to himself as he perused it. Now see my poor magic's operation, and trade consternation for contempt. Do you despise me?

FAUSTUS: Howe'er that may be. Good day, sir. I must take my leave.

MAGUS: Is time so short?

FAUSTUS: My child . . .

MAGUS: You note his cries have ceased.

FAUSTUS: Which need not trouble you. Adieu.

MAGUS: But tarry.

(FAUSTUS *starts toward the upstage doors to his home.*)

FAUSTUS: My family bids me.

MAGUS: They have no more need of you. They are long dead. You are forsworn, and your false oath has consigned them to Hell.

(*The* MAGUS *gestures, we hear the far-off ringing of a bell. The doors blow open violently to reveal, a scene of gray desolation, remnants of a building, a low mist upon the ground.*)

(FAUSTUS *turns from looking at the scene, to confront the* MAGUS *who, we find, has vanished.*)

ACT TWO

■ ■ ■

The portals which led to FAUSTUS's *home are opened, to reveal an expanse, upstage, of gray ruin.*

FAUSTUS *comes onto the stage, and looks around him. We hear a far-off bell ringing, and see an old man walking in the ruins.* FAUSTUS *turns to encounter him. We see it is his* FRIEND, *Fabian, now greatly aged.*

FAUSTUS: Where do we find ourselves?

FRIEND: I've often thought that it is Hell.

FAUSTUS: In truth?

FRIEND: I am grown so old it nor diverts nor profits me
to lie.

FAUSTUS: Have you grown old?

FRIEND: As you observe.

FAUSTUS: But we are of an age.

FRIEND: If you assert it.

FAUSTUS: Do you not know me?

FRIEND: Your voice is not unfamiliar, but perhaps it merely pleases.

FAUSTUS: Turn to me, look on me.

FRIEND: It would not profit, no, for I am blind.

FAUSTUS: Blind.

FRIEND: Yes.

FAUSTUS: What has befallen you? How came you to age?

FRIEND: Sir, I assure you, it was the passage of time.

FAUSTUS: (*Pause*) Are you mad? (*Pause*) Can you not answer me? Can you not aid me?

FRIEND: Not the first, sir, but, perhaps, the second.

FAUSTUS: I do not understand.

FRIEND: A sundial may offer information, but you remark, it withholds comment. (*Pause*)

FAUSTUS: Do you not know me?

FRIEND: I beg pardon.

FAUSTUS: I am Faustus.

FRIEND: Ask again if I am mad, I shall return the favor.

FAUSTUS: You suggest the debility is mine?

FRIEND: You have said that you are Faustus.

FAUSTUS: I am he.

FRIEND: What sane being would assert it?

FAUSTUS: I do not understand.

FRIEND: Then you are mad. (*He starts off.*) Or perverse, merely. I mean no offense. Whom could I dare offend?

FAUSTUS: Do not desert me.

FRIEND: Aid me then. Would you oblige, in description of the scene?

FAUSTUS: Near the conjunction of two roads.

FRIEND: I shall no further trouble you. (*The man walks off.*)

FAUSTUS: Stay, for I am unmoored; the pawl has clicked, the wheel come round, but I am baffled by the revolution. I beg you. Fabian. What is this charade? I do not understand its nature.

FRIEND: Nor I. Could I have creditably done so, would I not have resigned, long ago. But we understand, that is a crime, for which the criminals, self-punished, are additionally, damned. And their bones to an unmarked grave, at a crossroads.

FAUSTUS: Do I dream?

FRIEND: Should you, then I felicitate you.

FAUSTUS: Where is the family of Faustus?

FRIEND: Do I in fact remark your voice, sir? Or is it but th' association, summon'd by your questionings? But it is the same whate'er, and as the world draws in, as sight, sound, and action erode, what remains, but self-absorption? Where all is made fast to decay.

FAUSTUS: How came this to be so?

FRIEND: Through time and effort, as most things.

FAUSTUS: But how? The house is vanished, you are aged, yet time has not passed.

FRIEND: Then how am I grown old?

FAUSTUS: Indeed, who are but one day older than we found you yesterday.

FRIEND: Bless you, I must accept it, but, yesterday, I was old. I was old and blind.

FAUSTUS: You have gone blind from drink.

FRIEND: Thanks, good physician. But the cause was ne'er in doubt. (*Pause*) I wondered at the cure, though, those years. Til it grew plain, you see, like a far-off disturbing shape, which, upon approach, resolves itself, until we say, 'tis but a fault in the treeline.

FAUSTUS: And it resolved, to you, the cure for your disease . . . ?

FRIEND: 'Twas, of course, death. Which occupied decades of schooling. But I was blessed in my exemplars.

FAUSTUS: To wit?

FRIEND: I watched a family sicken and die, first the young lad, and then the woman, from grief. As she cried, over the years, for wisdom, then for fortitude, and, as any invalid, for this or that drug, in the hope it offered hope, 'til it was burned out of her.

FAUSTUS: Say on.

FRIEND: Her beauty, her desire, even for understanding, ebbed, 'til she was like the hollow tree, which at

length falls, of which we say, how not to've re-
marked, it died long ago. On the one hand, she had
a long life. On the other, poor angel, she lived it
anguished.

FAUSTUS: Where is the family lives here?

FRIEND: They have preceded us.

FAUSTUS: A prosperous family once controlled the land.

FRIEND: They own it still, though somewhat less of it.
Perhaps you'd aid me, sir, to seek that freehold.

FAUSTUS: Whose grave do you seek?

FRIEND: It were a crime, they say, to name it.

FAUSTUS: The boy.

FRIEND: The boy?

FAUSTUS: Faust's son.

FRIEND: Bless you, no, sir.

FAUSTUS: Then tell me he lives.

FRIEND: To please you, sir, I will. But in effect his crypt
lies yonder.

FAUSTUS: His crypt.

FRIEND: Untended these long years.

FAUSTUS: Not by his mother . . . ? (*Pause*)

FRIEND: One may not speak of her.

FAUSTUS: Why?

FRIEND: Have I not told you? (*Pause*)

FAUSTUS: Do you say she is dead?

FRIEND: You will forgive me, sir, my thoughts, absent direction, take their own lead.

FAUSTUS: Where is the woman's grave?

FRIEND: One may not know, sir, the grave of a suicide, who are damned to Hell. Do you feign ignorance of that gentle law? It extends e'en to those fair angels, on the earth, e'en those whose being cleansed and chastened. Whose each movement spoke of patience and grace, who were the anodyne to a life of dull disappointment, in whose very existence one found comfort for the, will I say, cruel impossibility of her possession. Fair, wasted angel. Self-slain, ne'er consummated love. O distance and O blessed death. Shall I requite your queries, sir? Those who impertinently usurp the divine, rest in an unmarked grave. What matter. When eternity wastes all.

FAUSTUS: Some say God is immortal.

FRIEND: Some say the sinful dead writhe in perpetual torment.

FAUSTUS: How did the boy die?

FRIEND: In an ague. Taken in a cold night. In a vain and protracted search, for another. In despair, at his abandonment.

FAUSTUS: Abandonment, you say.

FRIEND: By the man.

FAUSTUS: You will not say his name?

FRIEND: He died in grief, at his father's disappearance. It is a difficulty, as you may come to know, in age, to guard an undiminished hatred. After a time. That which once burned as molten iron. Becomes a mere fixed habit of the mind. Til one wakes one day, to find its very exercise an enervation.

FAUSTUS: Hatred.

FRIEND: Yes. But some does not die.

FAUSTUS: Must not all feeling change with time?

FRIEND: The truly wronged know otherwise.

FAUSTUS: Who has wronged you?

(*We hear the sound of a bell, and the man starts off.*)

FRIEND: I must go, for he hunts for me. Do you not find, we feel most beholden, sir, to those supplying an unnecessary service . . . ?

FAUSTUS: Who wronged you?

FRIEND: Who, indeed. He whom we indulged. To our cost. Our petted philosopher—who burned with the thirst for truth. Who betrayed those who trusted him, parsing their love to tribute and then to oblivion. Our sick creation. False friend, inconstant husband, engorged obscene digest of self-reference. We nurtured, for the entertainment, for the reflected glory—for which we shall not be forgiven. Who abided him, who, in his diffidence, subjected those he loved first to danger, then, to destruction, as I watched. I might have acted. I feared reproof, and classed it as respect for the proprieties. 'Twas not he, then, but I, sir, as you see, who was the criminal—to have subjected them to him. I must go. (*He starts off.*)

FAUSTUS: Stay: may I beg a service?

FRIEND: From one unfit as myself?

FAUSTUS: Where does she lie?

FRIEND: Act as I: Elect a spot, devote your obsequies, pray that it is her grave.

(*The* FRIEND *starts off.*)

FAUSTUS: (*To the departing* FRIEND) No, it offends sense. Say the man vanished, would not his family first misdoubt, accident, or illness, a man so beloved.

FRIEND: He fled in cowardice. Who would not brave public ridicule.

FAUSTUS: Ridicule?

FRIEND: Of his mis-envisioned, uncompleted work.

FAUSTUS: . . . uncompleted . . . ?

(*We hear the bell. The* FRIEND *goes off.*)

FAUSTUS: Am I unmanned to've lost the basic rudiments of reason?

(*The* MAGUS *appears onstage, carrying a large book.*)

FAUSTUS: Where is my family? (*Pause*) I have addressed you sir.

MAGUS: I've noted it.

FAUSTUS: Where is my family?

MAGUS: As is the destiny of all seed, they have been dispersed.

FAUSTUS: By what authority?

MAGUS: The less evolved would enquire by what mechanism. Good.

FAUSTUS: It is an illusion.

MAGUS: What is not? As have you not thrilled to teach us?

FAUSTUS: It is delusion, it is mesmeric projection, I lack the term to name the method, the motive is plain.

MAGUS: To wit?

FAUSTUS: A vicious act of envy. I have detractors, as must any prominent man. Indeed, I must have enemies. Have they employed you to drive me mad? To play upon my doubts? Have they told you of my shortcomings? Of my pride, of my unchecked imagination? Are you a tool of enmity? Of spite? Are you that inevitable assassin the elevated must fear, whose lack they themselves supply in counterpoise to their election . . . ? Are you madness . . . ? What are you? I conjure you . . .

DAVID MAMET

MAGUS: By what? I shall not press you.

FAUSTUS: Damn your impertinence, sir, and damn your illusion. I demand that you cease, restore, and revert all various aspects of the pantomime. The joke pales shockingly. And farewell, now farewell. Name and receive your payment, sir, for this diversion.

MAGUS: I have both named and received it.

FAUSTUS: It is a trick.

MAGUS: Pray accept this in compensation. (*He hands* FAUSTUS *the volume he has been holding in his hands.* FAUSTUS *takes it.*)

FAUSTUS: What pretends this to be?

MAGUS: It is your manuscript.

FAUSTUS: But it is aged . . .

MAGUS: . . . indeed . . .

(FAUSTUS *takes the book and reads.*)

FAUSTUS: "A discovery of the philosophic principles of Periodicity . . ."

(FAUSTUS *continues to leaf through the book.*)

FAUSTUS: The book is aged.

MAGUS: It is.

FAUSTUS: My friend, also, and decayed. (*Pause*) That which appears to be the remnant of my home bespeaks a passage of years.

MAGUS: From which you conclude? (*Pause*)

FAUSTUS: Where is my family?

MAGUS: Yes? Are you frightened?

FAUSTUS: Show them to me.

MAGUS: They are dead, you have murdered them.

FAUSTUS: Strong, striking verbiage, yet hardly discourse. You recur to causality. Then I have you, sir. For, name me the system of philosophy, or physics wherein effect may be without cause. For what freak do you suppose to punish me? Respond. I charge you.

MAGUS: You made a wager.

FAUSTUS: A wager? That is your plea? You rest the destruction of my happiness upon a bet? O, the wronged, are ever disadvantaged in debate. For the aggressor, may assert now this, now that, unfettered by fact, truth, or history. While the betrayed . . .

MAGUS: No more betrayed, but called to account. You contracted a wager.

FAUSTUS: I repudiate it.

MAGUS: One may repudiate the payment but of that which one holds in possession. Else it is called "chagrin."

FAUSTUS: Then I defy you, parse me the wager, sir, in justice.

MAGUS: But we delighted. To revile the advocates of justice; how we decried as puerile those who served; reason, and tradition, custom, law . . . Your work, your discourse, and, in fact your life were dedicated to the abrogation of commonalities.

FAUSTUS: Is it for this I am punished?

MAGUS: You are not punished, but foreclosed.

FAUSTUS: Then save me the gloss, and assert the forfeit. By your terms, sir, by your terms.

MAGUS: I will not foul the laws of fair debate.

FAUSTUS: So you have said. Then show me the default, sir, or restore all.

MAGUS: I name your magnum opus.

FAUSTUS: (*As he holds up the book*) It survives.

MAGUS: You still seek fame?

FAUSTUS: Yes, I am arrogant. Nay, arrogance itself, spare me the lesson. My work survives. You asserted it contained a flaw.

MAGUS: I did.

FAUSTUS: Indeed, a theft, which would disqualify it from renown save as a jest. A fool, a vicious, and unwarranted asseveration.

MAGUS: Which, were it to be established . . .

FAUSTUS: . . . I complete, which, were it proved supportable, would, would, would. (*Pause*) You taunted me. You dared me, as I understood, to take an oath. I took it as a jest.

MAGUS: You swore to the false, that which you staked was forfeit.

FAUSTUS: That my work was purloined? I defy you, sir, to suggest my work the subject of . . . yes, say, yes, incomprehension, yes, but impossibly of scorn. Let us grant you the passage of time. I cede you the truth of your illusion. Does my work not survive? (*He holds up the book.*)

MAGUS: But as a curio.

FAUSTUS: A *curio?* I call you to render justice.

MAGUS: Justice is blind, you have said she is also deaf.

FAUSTUS: But you are neither. You structure your chicanery in the mechanic mode: if this then that. Then *habeas deleatur:* show me the fault.

MAGUS: (*Of the book*) Read.

FAUSTUS: I am acquainted with it—I composed it. 'Tis mine entire. You charge me as a plagiarist. Show me the fault. I defy you.

MAGUS: Turn to the end.

FAUSTUS: (FAUSTUS *turns to the end.*) Indeed I shall.

MAGUS: Turn the last leaf and read.

FAUSTUS: Yes, yes, it is the final formula, and the apotheosis of the argument, where number is revealed but as progression.

MAGUS: Yes.

FAUSTUS: You feign I am undone in the conclusion? That it is debarred as purloined? It cannot be purloined, for it is pure imagination.

MAGUS: Turn the leaf:

(FAUSTUS *does so.*)

FAUSTUS: What viciousness is this? (*Reads*) "Three swift swallows in the summer sky, gone in the twinkling of an eye. One for the heart, one for the head, one for the lad who tarries abed." (*Pause*) It is the child's poem.

MAGUS: The manuscript appears under your name. Yet, you deny the conclusion's authorship.

FAUSTUS: The poem. How found it its way into my composition?

MAGUS: Take the page from your tunic. And read.

(FAUSTUS *does so and reads:*)

FAUSTUS: ". . . that number signifies not a quantity, but a progression . . ." This is not forfeit, sir, but mere prestidigitation.

MAGUS: Ah, sir, do you now conceive the world as a balance? Must one not then suppose one to read the scale? Which supposition you have dedicated your life, nay, in fact, this work, to disprove?

FAUSTUS: What power sends you as a plague, or are you an excrudescence of the general theme? Of envy. (*Pause*) What of my family?

MAGUS: They ran the extended limit of their course. They died. They perhaps continue, in a parallel world. As before. As e'er we ever met. Say it is true. Take comfort, and believe it.

FAUSTUS: Is it true?

MAGUS: Is it true? And you transfigured, from our brave savant, into a missish postulate who wished to know: the weight of the world, the run of time, the final construction of matter . . . as the poor fool who wished to understand grief. Your wish has been granted.

FAUSTUS: I could not have foreseen.

MAGUS: . . . *truly* . . . ? Then you should not have spoke. Or have your vaunted experiments in science taught you to pray that cause has no effect?

FAUSTUS: I understand. That I've offended, in some wise, or you, or, say if I go amiss, or, say, a tradition, or a power you represent. I pray to you to accept my regrets, and teach me how to particularize my homage. How shall I address you?

MAGUS: Well begun. Call me a merchant.

FAUSTUS: What do you seek?

MAGUS: As any merchant. That which in my realm is scarce.

FAUSTUS: What have you brought?

MAGUS: Say I have brought you fire.

FAUSTUS: Will not the gods be angry?

MAGUS: Suppose it their constant state. (*Pause*)

FAUSTUS: From whence do you come?

MAGUS: Shall you know more when I have told you?

FAUSTUS: Fit the response to my understanding.

MAGUS: Say from the future. Or the past. Say from another realm.

FAUSTUS: I am afraid.

MAGUS: You balked at the transmutation of a card. As the rock-dwelling savages recoiled at fire. You conflate: number, speech, thought, the mental and physical, and call your work complete. You are unfit e'en to frame the problem as a dog to speak; it lacks the mechanism. (*Pause*)

FAUSTUS: Sir . . . (*Pause*) Sir . . . Ah, sir. Ah, good sir. Ah worthy preceptor, to school in atonement. To strip from me, the prop of self-regard. To offer that omnipotent admixture of grief and self-humiliation . . .

MAGUS: Whom do you think confronts you? (*Pause*) You hesitate.

FAUSTUS: Yes.

MAGUS: From confusion?

FAUSTUS: No. No, from . . . (*Pause*)

MAGUS: You must supply the word.

FAUSTUS: From awe. (*Pause*)

MAGUS: I attend . . . (*Pause*)

FAUSTUS: We have heard voices. In the dark. In childhood, in extremity. Perhaps at death . . . we have construed them as . . . (*Pause*) those promptings religion derogates as survival of savagery. Of ancient, superceded nature . . .

MAGUS: The power of which you speak. Does it possess a name?

FAUSTUS: What do you want of me?

MAGUS: I await your suggestion.

FAUSTUS: No, the gods, would damn me, can it be, for the ignorance of a formula?

MAGUS: Upon what then, should they rely?

FAUSTUS: Upon . . . upon the evidence, say of my contrition.

MAGUS: What leads you to believe they prefer it to the entertainment of your pain?

FAUSTUS: I cannot credit it.

MAGUS: Are they, then, in contradistinction to your avowed thesis, omniscient and benign?

FAUSTUS: My works are empty, I abjure them. They are the toy of an overfed mind.

MAGUS: Truly?

FAUSTUS: I have been wrong. In which I am but human. God spare me. My life was not without merit.

MAGUS: What merit might that be?

FAUSTUS: My family . . . My wife loved me, my child.

MAGUS: He loved you?

FAUSTUS: He penned me a poem.

MAGUS: Did you not derogate it?

FAUSTUS: Did I? Then may God forgive me.

MAGUS: Read it to me . . .

FAUSTUS: . . . Why?

MAGUS: To conflate the two.

FAUSTUS: I confess, the two productions are one, my manuscript, and the child's poem. Yes. I am taught. His is superior.

MAGUS: Why?

FAUSTUS: His . . . His was writ in love. I . . .

MAGUS: Confess—

FAUSTUS: I . . . shall confess . . . to my petted self-adoration. To coward miching, to entertainment of the establishment which I was licensed to decry. I was a whore, corrupt for all time, and unfit for any purpose greater than debauchery.

MAGUS: You divert, but fail to convince of your sincerity. Confess.

FAUSTUS: To what end?

MAGUS: To the end that you cease to enquire, for my entertainment, for no end at all.

FAUSTUS: God help me.

MAGUS: God spare me, the frightened call, and confect endless, elaborate self-castigation. Spared, they employ reprieve in sin. Thus coupling cowardice to comedy.

FAUSTUS: Until . . . ?

MAGUS: Shall we turn to the coda? Shall we exhibit those upon whom you practiced your charade? Shall we show you your family?

FAUSTUS: You have said they are dead.

MAGUS: As if they never lived, or dwelt, solely in your imagination. (*Pause*) Or the imagination of another.

FAUSTUS: Of what other?

MAGUS: Shall I tell you? (*Pause*)

FAUSTUS: Show me my family.

MAGUS: Your son's in heaven, and beyond my sway.

FAUSTUS: My wife?

MAGUS: She is damned as a suicide—with *her* you may be reunited.

FAUSTUS: Yes, I see.

MAGUS: So you perceive the tariff. (*Pause*)

FAUSTUS: Sir, you have seduced me, you have played upon
my weakness. You indict me of hypocrisy, of greed,
of self-blind egoism; your victory makes good your
claim. You now taunt me with cowardice. Where I
confront you. I wish to see my wife.

MAGUS: Nothing may be had for nothing.

FAUSTUS: Yes, merchant—yes, I see that for which you
have come. I close the bargain. And am shed of you.
Give me the dagger.

MAGUS: In truth, sir, then you do impress.

FAUSTUS: Indeed I care not. Give me the knife.

(*The* MAGUS *hands* FAUSTUS *the dirk. The* MAGUS *retires
upstage, leaving* FAUSTUS *alone, as the doors close.*)

FAUSTUS: Omnipotent winter which alone reveals the
underlying structure of the land—he who has sought
beauty in the ruined, how otherwise than reap this
empty, sad, perpetual requital. Who sickens to the
point where wisdom lies with the ironmonger.
Here is damnation, then. And there's an end to
hypocrisy . . .

(*He puts the knife to his throat. Upstage the doors blow open to reveal Hell, from which we see appear* FAUSTUS's WIFE, *in torn, soot-blackened garments. Pause. As* FAUSTUS *looks at his* WIFE:)

FAUSTUS: My wife, my angel wife.

(FAUSTUS *hesitates. The* MAGUS *appears at his side.*)

MAGUS: You may continue.

FAUSTUS: How may I frame my contrition? . . . For what may I beg . . . ?

MAGUS: For pardon . . . ?

FAUSTUS: May I beg for pardon?

MAGUS: You hesitate.

FAUSTUS: I would not waste the least of her attention. I beg the one moment to compose the speech.

MAGUS: It makes no odds, as she cannot hear. We to her are less than phantoms. (*Pause*)

WIFE: It is an adamantine monument. To sin for surely it must be the fruit of crime though what I know not to have elected that course which concludes in such calamity. Or were it better never to have lived? Or spent a life barren and envious. For could not envy

be borne? You were envious. Your theme was cov-
etousness—and self-worship.

FAUSTUS: Whom does she address?

MAGUS: As you suspect.

WIFE: You envied all fame but your own, and basked in the
self-awarded mantle of simplicity. And we who loved,
indulged you. To your cost. As the petted dog, pierces
our assumed severity. He understands innocuous
chastisement as praise. And seeks it. By soiling his
home. You strove for fame. For the delusion of pop-
ular love. My son my son, sacrifice to a profligate,
absconding father . . . And I chose you. Fool, wicked
fool. Perpetually damned mother—for what sin
was I coupled to you in penance? Unnatural vicious
father. How odd. When devotion engulfed you.

FAUSTUS: My wife.

WIFE: This is a mother's plaint. Formed as a fugue: of
pride and fear, regret and uncertainty. It is the most
ancient song of conquest. For women conquer but
the once, and then are self-schooled. Poor story. To
live supine. First to conceive, and then to bear. At
long last only licensed to revolve, our face to the
ground. But to weep. (*We hear the pealing of the
bell.*) . . . Yes, I attend . . .

MAGUS: See how the circularity augments the grief.

WIFE: Fool woman who was content with little. With so little . . . (*The* WIFE *exits.*)

MAGUS: Indeed, dashing all barriers to its intensification. The dropped stone stops at earth; gluttony brings repletion, the libertine copulates but to debility, in each the cure grows apace with the malady. It is a law. In all things but grief.

FAUSTUS: Grief must find a rest.

MAGUS: Behold the exception. She is a suicide, and lives forever. A self-perpetuating energy, increased in moment through sheer force of contemplation. Must we not stand unabashed, to receive whate'er of insight, awe, or entertainment our various natures may propose.

FAUSTUS: God Damn You.

MAGUS: Blasphemy and prayer are one. An appeal, thus an assertion of a superior power. Do you acknowledge it? I ask. Do you, at length, sense the true meaning of confession?

FAUSTUS: I wish to see my son.

MAGUS: You have bartered and been paid.

FAUSTUS: I call upon God . . .

MAGUS: And I invite you to denounce God.

FAUSTUS: I denounce the Devil, in all of his undertakings. I convict myself, of a life of heresy. My every thought idolatrous, all my devotions sham, and homage to a false god. I disclaim them, I renounce every thought, exhortation, observance, devotion, and deed as sin and prostrate myself, helpless, before the One True God. It cannot lack precedent. Grant me the power to frame my contrition. Dear God, hear my prayer.

MAGUS: Why should a god prefer your prayers to your agony?

FAUSTUS: Let that stand as my offering: the anguish of a contrite heart. I beg for recision of my child's death, of my wife's suffering. God, who can read my heart, mighty judge, with no deeds to plead for him, here stands your servant, shriven, at last, to your will. Hear me.

MAGUS: The voices of the Damned may not be heard above.

FAUSTUS: I then plead for an intercessor. To one consecrated to Heaven. To speak for me. I call upon my son. My son, an angel.

MAGUS: Do not name him.

FAUSTUS: Then there exists that intuited mercy. Yes. To which your speech testifies. My son, untouched by sin, unimplicated, blameless. Is there not that bond?

Stronger than death—a sweet, unending child's love, oh son. Say that you hear my prayer.

(*The drop parts behind* FAUSTUS *to now reveal Heaven, where we find* FAUSTUS'*s* SON.)

CHILD: I hear you . . .

(FAUSTUS *turns to see his* SON, *and advances to him.*)

FAUSTUS: O blessed Child, how the sweet moment stuns me to chastisement. Dear Child. Oh, son, of my heart, exult the power which vouchsafed this interview. Oh, son. Intercede for me.

CHILD: Intercede . . .

FAUSTUS: For a poor penitent. Who implores your forgiveness. Plead for me, not for my worth, I have none. For yours. Forward your merit in my case. Bear my petition.

CHILD: Ah, that is why you have appeared today.

FAUSTUS: . . . today.

CHILD: Today is the day of atonement.

FAUSTUS: Of atonement . . .

CHILD: You bear a petition.

FAUSTUS: I do.

CHILD: Say it to me.

FAUSTUS: Yes, I shall—my angel—that my wife, that my
child, and myself may return, to the earth, whole,
and restored, as before.

CHILD: Whole and restored.

FAUSTUS: Bear my plea. Best of the two worlds. Through
all my criminal confusion one truth endured, un-
doubted, and pure. That of your love—pity me, and
preach your benignity in my cause on high.

CHILD: I shall.

FAUSTUS: Praise God—Oh, praise God.

CHILD: But to plead in the cause of whom? (*Pause*)

FAUSTUS: Can you not know me?

CHILD: How should I know you? (*Pause*) Am I not endless
blessed?

FAUSTUS: You are.

CHILD: In what could eternal blessing consist save in
oblivion? (*Pause*)

FAUSTUS: . . . my son.

CHILD: Am I your son?

FAUSTUS: Surely there's a residuary memory. An ineradicable memory.

CHILD: Of?

FAUSTUS: Of love. Between a father and son. Which transcends death. I know it. In my soul. It is an attribute of God. Our love.

CHILD: And did I love you?

FAUSTUS: Oh, my son.

CHILD: Tell me of love.

FAUSTUS: . . . no, can you doubt me?

CHILD: I am unfitted to perceive duplicity. I ask as for a gift.

FAUSTUS: Yes, I shall tell you of love.

CHILD: In this particular: the better to fit me to plead your case. It is the hour of audience.

FAUSTUS: Yes.

CHILD: When the bell toll, and until the bell cease. And the gates have closed.

FAUSTUS: A man, a family begs to be reunited. In love . . . you wrote of it.

CHILD: Tell me.

FAUSTUS: You wrote a poem. You composed me a poem. Bear it on high. Attend:

> *"Heavy Heavy the Hired man*
> *Weary, how weary the willing hand . . ."*

CHILD: But this is a sad recital.

FAUSTUS: 'Tis but the preamble.

CHILD: It awakens memory.

FAUSTUS: Yes.

CHILD: But, 'tis memory of pain.

FAUSTUS: Of pain . . .

CHILD: Yes . . .

FAUSTUS: No, but let me continue.

CHILD: 'Tis a sad song.

FAUSTUS: It turns. Wait . . . see: at the end . . .

CHILD: You say it speaks of love.

FAUSTUS: It does.

CHILD: Complete it for me. (*Pause*) Why do you hesitate? (*Pause. We hear a bell tolling.*) I must go. It is the hour of intercession. Until the bell cease. Give me the poem, and it shall plead for you.

FAUSTUS: Wait . . . (*The* CHILD *begins to disappear. The* MAGUS *appears.*)

FAUSTUS: Return me my book.

MAGUS: You have renounced it.

FAUSTUS: Give me the poem.

MAGUS: You remark I bid you peruse it.

FAUSTUS: I am summoned to approach the Throne.

MAGUS: And you are debarred. (*Pause*) The biddable ape, whose antics delight in their travesty of understanding. His fist closed tight around the nut in the glass jar. He rallies heaven for an explanation. He invokes his merit and his ancestry. See now his simian face contort in travesty of philosophic consternation. You wonder why you are pursued? For entertainment.

FAUSTUS: I am to you but a diversion.

MAGUS: In fine.

FAUSTUS: Then pay me.

MAGUS: Pay you?

FAUSTUS: For the one thing's true, in heaven or hell, and by your own admission, one must pay for entertainment. Pay me, then, who has entertained you. Give me my poem. Give me my poem.

MAGUS: Who has vexed me since you first besought me.

(FAUSTUS *is handed the poem—starts to leave.*)

FAUSTUS: I ne'er besought you, sir, my friend besought you.

MAGUS: I was summoned by your o'erweening pride.

FAUSTUS: My pride . . .

MAGUS: And your impertinence.

FAUSTUS: And have I not prevailed?

MAGUS: Then go boast of your victory. I tire of you.

FAUSTUS: Or do you fear me.

MAGUS: . . . fear you . . .

FAUSTUS: Or do I see, in your capitulation, a man taken at his word. His word ratified by the respect, which attends his approach.

(*A bell rings.*)

MAGUS: The gates are closing.

FAUSTUS: And that you, with your trumpery scorn, seek to dismiss him who had bested you. Who wrenched from you license to see heav'n and hell and walk free. Who has Probed the Center.

(*A bell rings.*)

MAGUS: . . . to have found . . . ?

FAUSTUS: . . . the Secret Engine of the World. O sacred light, the signs congeal, you are come to induct me . . .

(*A bell rings.*)

MAGUS: The gates are closing.

FAUSTUS: I am become as God.

MAGUS: And now the gates are closed.

FAUSTUS: I am completed.

MAGUS: As, My Lord, am I.